The Coolest Pets

Horses and Ponies

Anne O'Daly

KidHaven PUBLISHING

Published in 2024 by
KidHaven Publishing, an Imprint of Greenhaven Publishing, LLC
2544 Clinton St., Buffalo, NY 14224

Portions of this work were originally authored by Dawn Titmus and published as *Horses and Ponies.*
All new material this edition authored by Anne O'Daly.

Design Manager: Keith Davis
Picture Manager: Sophie Mortimer

Photo Credits:
Front Cover: Shutterstock: Eric Isselee all photographs.
Interior: Dreamstime: Pat Olson 9t; iStock: Clark and Company 27t, cynoclub 7bl, GlobalIP 18-19, 22-23, grigoritako 4bl, Groomee 17t, mari_art 23b, matthewleesdixon 29b, Mlenny 19b, Marilyn Nieves 9b, olgaIT 14, Roxanne Roy 21b, tunart 19t, wavebreakmedia 17b; Shutterstock: ahturner 8r, anakondasp 8b, Alla Berlezova 21t, Ad van Brunschot 6br, Callipso 1, 24-25, Marie Charouzova 29tl, cynoclub 4-5, 7br, Ewais 6-7, Ian Fletcher 13t, IFotokostic 15t, Bianca Grueneberg 10-11, Jari Hindstroem 15b, index74 16, Grigorita Ko 29c, Andrzej Kubik 27b, lofio69 18, lucag_g 23t, mariait 26-27, Sari O'Neal 6bl, 10, Nigel Baker Photography 25t, Maralee Park 7bc, pirita 12t, 13b, racorn 12b, wavebreakmedia 11, Vera Zinkova 20-21, zuzule 25b.
Key: t=top, b=bottom, c=center, l=left, r=right

Cataloging-in-Publication Data

Names: O'Daly, Anne
Title: Horses and ponies / Anne O'Daly.
Description: Buffalo, New York : Kidhaven Publishing, 2024. |
Series: The coolest pets| Includes index and glossary
Identifiers: ISBN 9781534545441 (pbk) | ISBN 9781534545458 (library bound) | ISBN 9781534545465 (ebook)
Subjects: LCSH: Horses-- Juvenile literature | Ponies--Juvenile literature |Pets--Juvenile literature
Classification: LCC SF302 O33 2024 | DDC 636.1--dc23

Manufactured in the United States of America

CPSIA compliance information: Batch #CSKH24: For further information contact Greenhaven Publishing LLC at 1-844-317-7404.

Please visit our website, www.greenhavenpublishing.com.
For a free color catalog of all our high-quality books, call toll free 1-844-317-7404 or fax 1-844-317-7405.

Find us on

Contents

Choosing a Horse or Pony

Horses and ponies are intelligent animals and can be great to own. However, they need a lot more care and commitment than many other pets.

Measure Up!

The height of a horse or pony is measured in hands. One hand is 4 inches (10 cm). Ponies are smaller than 14 and a half hands, or 58 inches (1.47 m). Horses and ponies can live for 30 years.

Hard Work

Looking after a horse or pony takes time and effort. They need to be fed, watered, groomed, and exercised every day. Horses and ponies also need visits from the vet and farrier. Think carefully about whether you have the time and energy to spare.

Checklist

- Do you have space for a horse or pony?
- Do you have time to look after and exercise a horse or pony every day?
- Can your family afford to keep a horse or pony?

Space to Roam

Horses and ponies need plenty of space to graze and roam. You will need to provide shelter, too. If you have a paddock, you may choose to keep your pet at home. Another option is to pay to keep your horse at a stable.

Money

It is costly to keep a horse or pony. As well as food and stabling, you will need equipment for grooming and riding. There will also be vet and farrier bills to pay.

Next Steps

Horses and ponies make great pets, but it is important to think carefully before owning one. This book describes the basics of caring for horses and ponies and looks at four popular breeds. Try your hand at making a "stained glass" horse window. You will also find some fascinating facts about our equine friends!

Getting Started

If you've decided to buy a horse or pony, you will need special equipment to care for it properly. Grooming tools keep your horse clean. You will also need stable equipment and riding gear.

Grooming

Different types of brushes and combs are used for grooming a horse. The mane and tail need to be groomed regularly. Special brushes and combs are used to polish the horse's coat. You will also need a hoof pick to remove stones from the hooves.

Checklist

- Grooming brushes and combs.
- Hoof pick.
- Feed tub and water bucket.
- Cleaning equipment for the barn.
- Tack: halter, lead rope, saddle, saddle pad, and bridle.
- Hard helmet, riding boots, and gloves.

Gear and Tack

Your horse will need a saddle, saddle pad or blanket, and a bridle. Western saddles are bigger and heavier than English saddles. English saddles have metal stirrups, while western saddles have leather ones. Always wear a helmet when riding. You also need boots that have at least a 1-inch (2.5 cm) heel to stop your feet from slipping through the stirrups. Wearing gloves protects your hands and prevents the reins from slipping.

For the Stable

If you keep your pet at home, you will need a feed tub and water trough or buckets, as well as hay nets or hay racks. The stall has to be cleaned out regularly, so you will also need a pitchfork, stable broom, wheelbarrow, and manure fork.

Safety Tips

Learning about horse behavior will help keep you safe. Sensible clothing and the right equipment are important, too. Take your time and follow some basic safety rules.

Leading and Tying

Learn how to put a halter and rope on a horse safely. Ask an experienced rider to show you if you're not sure. When leading a horse, walk by its neck or shoulder. To turn the horse, turn it away from you and walk around it. Never wrap the lead rope around your hand or arm. If your horse suddenly pulls, your hand or arm may become trapped. If you need to tether, or tie up, your horse while you groom it, tie it to a tie ring or strong post.

Hard Hat and Boots

When you ride, always wear a helmet and riding boots. Wearing gloves helps prevent the reins slipping in your hands. Wear hard-toed boots around horses. A horse stepping on your foot will hurt. Clean the tack regularly and check it is safe.

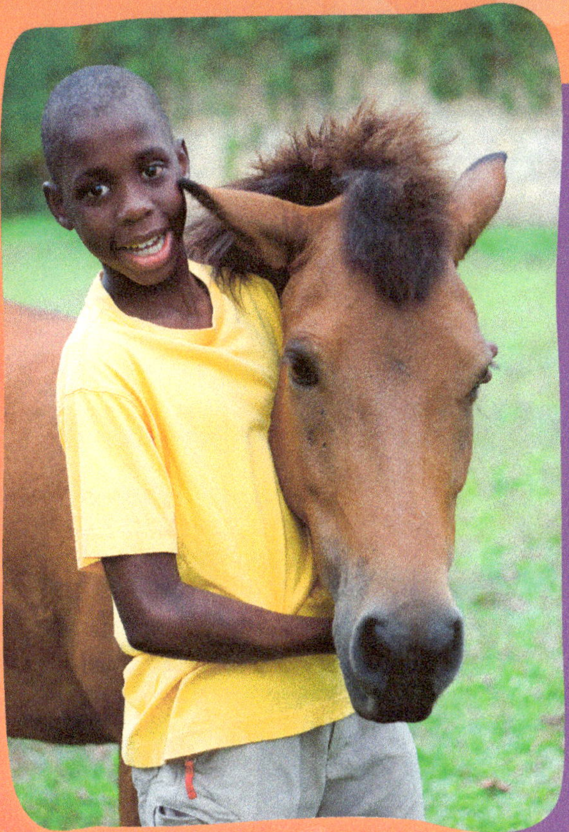

Body Language

Learn to understand your pet's body language. A horse that is swishing its tail or turning its rump toward you is showing it is unhappy and may kick. Horses have blind spots right in front and behind them. Touch a horse on its shoulder or neck, not its nose. Never surprise a horse or approach it from behind. It may kick if it's surprised. When grooming the tail, stand to the side of the horse, not right behind it. Let it know what you're doing by touching it firmly and talking to it. Be calm and never get angry with a horse or pony.

Equipment Checks

Check that the equipment you're using is not worn or broken. Look for fraying lead ropes or halters that could break when your horse is tied up. Always check the girth is secured properly before you mount your horse. If it's loose, the saddle may slip and you could fall off!

Food and Drink

Horses and ponies need a well-balanced diet to stay fit and healthy. Their stomachs are small, so they feed little and often.

Fresh Water

Horses need plenty of fresh water. They can drink between 10 to 12 gallons (38 to 45 liters) of water a day. If you live in an area with cold winters, use a water heater or heated buckets to stop ice forming on the water.

Eats Like a Horse!

Horses eat a lot! The average-sized horse eats about 15 to 20 pounds (7 to 9.5 kg) of food every day. Exactly how much your horse needs depends on its size and how much activity it does. A horse that is not being ridden or worked needs less food than a very active horse, such as a racehorse.

Poison

Some plants are poisonous for horses. Plants such as yew, bracken fern, dogbane, and milkweed should be removed from your horse's pasture. Contact your county extension office for information about which poisonous plants grow in your county.

Hay and Grain

Feed your horse or pony at least three times a day. Their diet should be mainly forage, such as alfalfa, grass hay, or pasture. The natural food of horses and ponies is grass. Many horses get all they need just from grazing in a pasture. Stall horses need to have hay to munch on. Most horses also need grain. Grain is made from oats, corn, bran, or barley. Give your horse small amounts of grain frequently rather than one large meal.

Cleaning and Grooming

Clean out your horse's stall at least once a day. Daily grooming will keep your pet's coat in good condition. Always groom before and after riding.

Brushing and Grooming

Make sure your horse is safely tied up. Clean out the hooves using a hoof pick. Use a curry comb or mitt to remove dead hair and dirt from the coat moving with strong, circular strokes. This massages the skin and releases natural oils, making the coat shine. Use a dandy brush to flick off the dirt, then finish off with a body brush to make the coat glossy.

Detangle

The mane and tail can become tangled. Use a brush or comb to gently tease out the tangles, or use your fingers to detangle before you start brushing. Begin at the end of the tail and work your way up. Stand to the side so you can't get kicked. Grooming sprays can also help untangle mane and tail hair.

Cleaning Up

Use a pitchfork or shovel to remove manure and wet bedding every day. Replace the soiled bedding with clean bedding. Sweep up straw or wood shavings. Completely clean out the stall once a week and replace all the bedding.

Finishing Touches

Use a damp sponge or soft cloth to gently clean your horse's ears, eyes, and nose. Check the ears for dirt or grass seeds. Go slowly, as some horses don't like their ears being touched. Finally, use the cloth or sponge to clean the area under the tail, standing to the side so you don't get kicked.

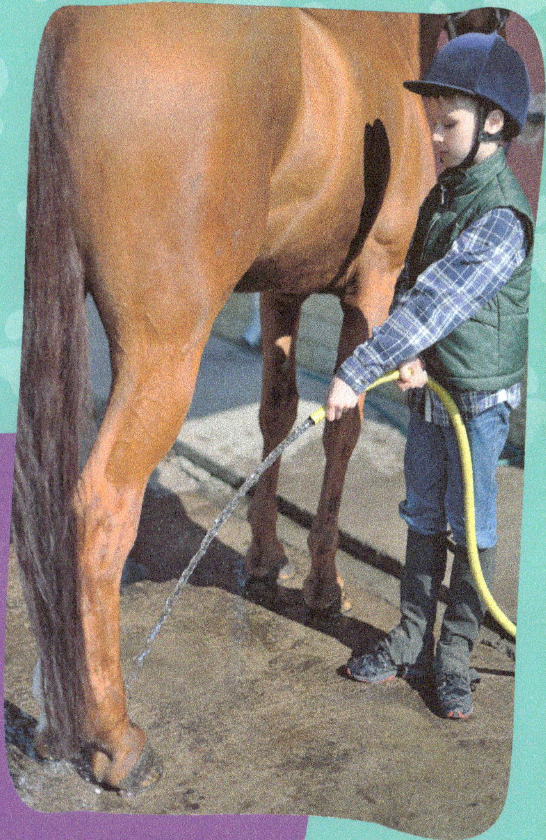

Bathtime

If you are taking your horse to a show, wash it a few days before the event. It will give the coat time to get its glossy sheen back. Use a small amount of special shampoo. Be careful not to spray water directly into your horse's face. Dry your horse with a sweat scraper and towels, then walk it around for a few minutes to finish drying, or cover it with a thin blanket.

Exercise and Shelter

Horses and ponies need plenty of space to exercise. If they are kept outdoors, they will need a place to shelter from the weather. You can exercise your horse by riding, driving, or longeing.

Living Outdoors

If your horse or pony lives on outdoor pasture, it can exercise as much as it likes. Horses are naturally herd animals, so it will be happier if there are other horses on the same pasture. They will need shelter from the sun in summer and from the wind, rain, and cold in winter. A small three-sided shed should provide them with enough shelter.

Pen or Paddock

Some horses live in a pen or paddock. A paddock is a small field or pasture. A pen is an outside space that should ideally be at least 24 by 24 feet (7.3 by 7.3 m). Horses in a large pen or paddock can exercise by themselves, but they will need to have some extra exercise three or four times a week.

Indoor Stall

The size of the stall you need depends on the size of your horse or pony. Most horses will be happy in a stall that is 12 by 10 feet (3.5 by 3 m). Ponies are comfortable in smaller stalls. Horses that live in a stall need to be exercised every day. You can turn your horse out to pasture or a paddock for exercise. Follow this with at least one hour a day of riding, driving, or longeing.

Keeping Healthy

Good foods and exercise will help keep your pet healthy. But all animals get sick sometimes and you may need to call a vet. Try to find one that specializes in horses and ponies.

Daily Checks

Knowing how your horse behaves when it's healthy helps you spot the signs when it's sick. A healthy horse looks alert with bright eyes and holds the ears forward. Grooming is a good time to check for any lumps or injuries on your horse. Notice how it is standing. A horse holding up a leg may be lame. Does your horse limp when it moves or take small steps? Call the vet if you think your horse may be lame.

Colic

Horses and ponies cannot throw up if they eat poison or too much food. They get a bad stomachache, called colic, if something has upset their stomach. Your pet might have colic if it is restless, lying down and rolling over, or looking at its sides. Call the vet if you think your pet has colic.

Signs of Sickness

- Your pet is not eating its food or drinking water.
- Its eyes are dull or it looks nervous.
- It is rolling around on the ground (colic).
- It is limping or taking small, awkward steps (lameness).

Hoof Care

Check your horse's hooves every day for dirt or loose shoes. Like fingernails, hooves keep growing. They will need to be trimmed by a farrier every six to eight weeks. Don't let your horse stand in water or a wet stall for long. Wet hooves may split and break.

Parasites

All horses have worms that live inside their bodies. Most horses need a deworming treatment every two months. Watch out for tiny yellow botfly eggs on your horse. Remove the eggs with a bot block or a blunt pocket knife. Also have your vet check your horse for ticks and lice.

In the Wild

Horses and ponies belong to the same family as asses, donkeys, and zebras. Wild horses once lived all over the world. About 6,000 years ago, people domesticated horses.

Przewalski's Horse

The Przewalski's horse comes from Mongolia and China, in Asia. It became extinct in the wild. Some horses were kept and bred in captivity. They were set free in nature reserves in Mongolia and China. Today, there are about 2,000 Przewalski's horses in reserves in Asia and Europe.

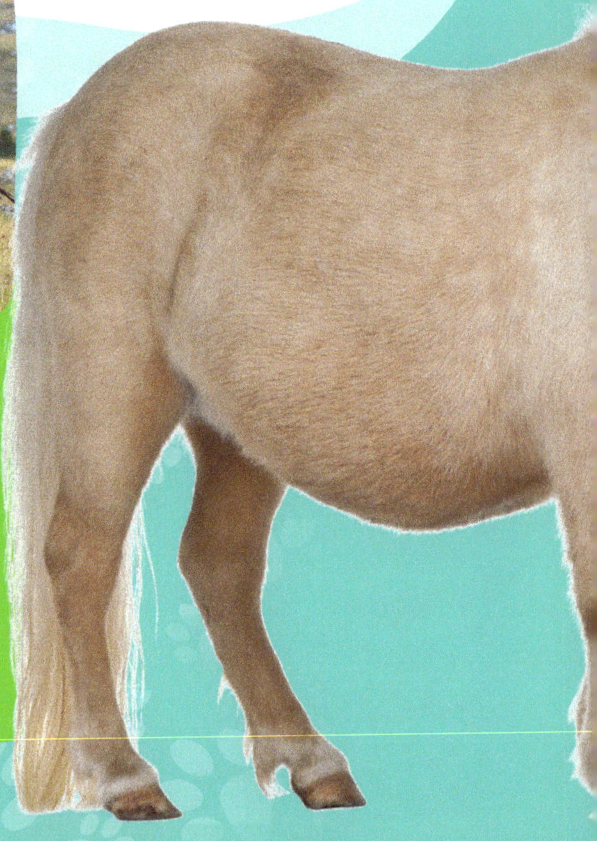

Herds of Horses

Horses live in herds in the wild. Usually, there is a stallion with a group of mares and their foals. When colts are about two or three years old, the stallion drives them away from the herd. The colts may band together until they start their own herds.

Semi-wild Horse

Some horses are semi-wild. They have owners but are left to roam free most of the time. Shetland ponies (left) live semi-wild on the Shetland Islands, off the north coast of Scotland. Camargue horses in southern France have a semi-wild life. Semi-wild horses also live in England, Germany, and Norway.

Mustangs and Brumbies

Mustangs (right) and brumbies are feral horses. They are descended from domestic horses that were turned loose or escaped into the wild. Mustangs are descended from Spanish horses that were introduced to the Americas in the 1500s. Brumbies live in Australia. They are descended from horses the British first took to Australia in 1788.

Quarter Horse

The American quarter horse is the most popular breed in the United States. Its name comes from the fact that it was faster than other horse breeds in races of a quarter mile (400 m) or less.

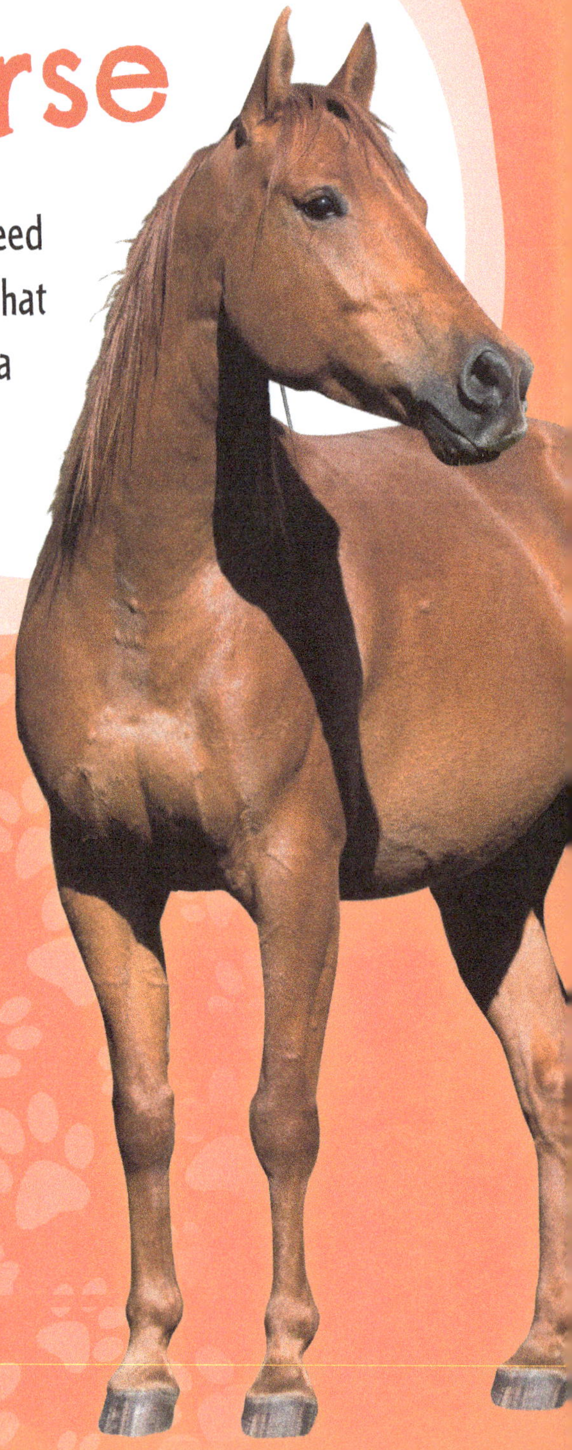

The American quarter horse is gentle and intelligent.

Where in the World?

The American quarter horse was first bred by settlers in the 1800s in what is now the United States. In the American West, the quarter horse was used as a ranch horse by cowboys and as a racing horse.

Pet Care

Quarter horses are excellent riding, race, and show horses. They are suited to owners who have limited experience.

* Quarter horses do well on a simple diet of hay.
* Don't overfeed your pet. Quarter horses put on weight easily.

Profile

The quarter horse stands between 14.3 and 16 hands high. It comes in a range of colors, including bay, chestnut, and white. It has a strong, muscular body and excels in rodeo events. Quarter horses can live for up to 30 years.

Appaloosa

The Appaloosa is instantly recognizable from its coat of dark or white spots. It is a strong, gentle, intelligent animal.

Where in the World?

The Nez Perce Native Americans first bred Appaloosas in the 1700s. The Appaloosa was recognized as a breed in 1938. It is the state horse of Idaho.

The leopard spot Appaloosa has a white body with dark spots.

Pet Care

Appaloosas are usually calm and reliable. They are considered to be good horses for children to ride.

* They can live happily on pasture or in a barn or box stall.
* Appaloosas can be prone to sunburn. Use a good sunblock on pink or white areas of their muzzle.

Profile

Appaloosas stand between 14.2 and 15.2 hands high. They can have spots over all of their body or part of it. They have striped hooves, and the whites of their eyes are visible. The base coat comes in a range of colors, including black, bay, and gray. The Appaloosa can live for up to 30 years.

Welsh Pony

Welsh ponies are intelligent, tough, and full of personality. The breed includes four types, from the small and dainty Welsh mountain pony to the strong Welsh cob.

Where in the World?

Welsh ponies are from the mountains of Wales, in the United Kingdom. Sure-footed and strong, they were used on farms and to pull carts in coal mines. Today, they are a popular riding pony.

The Welsh pony has an arched neck and strong legs.

Pet Care

Welsh ponies are versatile. They are natural jumpers, good at showing, and can also pull carts and traps.

* These ponies are tough enough to stay outside all year round.
* Welsh ponies developed to graze on poor, mountainous land. Too much food, or grass that is too rich, can lead to health problems.

Profile

Welsh ponies have pretty faces with almond-shaped eyes. The four types come in a range of colors. The smallest is the mountain pony. The Welsh pony is bigger and makes a good riding pony. The two largest types are the Welsh pony cob and the Welsh horse cob.

Arabian

The beautiful Arabian is one of the oldest horse breeds in the world.

Where in the World?

The Arabian developed from wild horses in the deserts of western Asia. It was one of the first breeds to be domesticated, more than 3,000 years ago. Today, Arabian horses are kept all around the world.

The Arabian has a beautifully curved face and an arched neck.

Pet Care

The Arabian is known for its speed and stamina. It is friendly and intelligent, but best for experienced riders.

- Arabians eat fresh grass and good quality hay. They need access to fresh water.
- Groom regularly to keep the coat in good condition.

Profile

Arabian, or Arab, horses stand between 14.1 and 15.1 hands. They have a delicate head, with large eyes and nostrils. Coat colors include black, brown, and gray. Whatever the color of the coat, the skin underneath is black. The mane and tail are silky, and the tail is held high compared to other breeds. Arabians were used to develop other breeds, including the quarter horse. The typical lifespan is 20 to 30 years.

Easy-to-Make

Colorful Window

Use colored tissue paper and construction paper to make a "stained glass" window with a horse's head for your bedroom.

You Will Need:

* Scissors
* Waxed paper
* Colored tissue paper
* Glue
* Black construction paper
* Tape (optional)

1 Ask an adult to find you a picture of a solid black horse head. You can find one at a clip art site.

2 Print the horse head and carefully cut it out.

3 Cut out a piece of waxed paper that is large enough for your horse head to fit on.

4 Tear colored tissue paper into long strips or small squares.

5 Glue the tissue paper onto the waxed paper. Overlap the pieces to make a pretty background.

6 Put the horse head on top of the tissue paper. When you are happy with the position, glue it in place.

7 Cut four strips of black construction paper to make a frame for your window. Glue or tape the corners together. Then glue the strips around your window.

Put your window in front of a light or tape it onto your bedroom window so the light shines through.

Fun Facts

Horses' teeth keep growing and are worn down by chewing. The shape and angle of a horse's teeth change as it ages. Vets can estimate a horse's age by looking at the shape and angle of its teeth.

Horses use their ears, eyes, and nostrils to show how they feel. They sniff each other's noses to say hello. They also express their feelings through their tail. Swishing the tail up and down can mean that the horse is annoyed.

Usually, horses in a herd don't all lie down at the same time. At least one horse stays standing to be lookout and warn the others of any danger.

In the United States, there are about 1.75 million workhorses. Among other jobs, they work on farms, in rodeos, and with police.

Horses have almost 360-degree vision. They have blind spots directly in front and behind them.

Horses have a better sense of hearing than humans. They can turn their ears around toward sounds coming from different directions.

Horses use different sounds to communicate. They whinny or neigh when they meet or leave another horse. Stallions roar loudly when they are seeking a mate. Horses snort to warn other horses of danger.

Horses are used in therapy. Interacting with a horse helps people build trust and self-confidence, improve communication, and learn new skills.

Glossary

alfalfa plant grown for hay.

blind spot area that the eye cannot see.

bot block rough stone used to remove botfly eggs from horse's hair.

botfly type of fly that lives inside some mammals before it becomes an adult and can fly.

captivity the state of being kept by people, not free.

colt young male horse.

descended come from the same family.

domesticated formerly wild animals that now live with people.

dominant controlling others.

driving (of horses) pulling a cart or carriage.

equestrian relating to riding.

equine relating to horses.

farrier person who cares for and shoes horses' hooves.

feral describes an animal that has escaped and become wild.

forage grasses and other plants eaten by animals.

girth strap to hold a saddle on a horse's back.

lice small insects that live on the bodies of animals and people.

longeing exercising a horse on a long rein or strap.

mare female horse.

muzzle jaws and nose of an animal.

paddock small field where animals are kept.

stallion male horse.

sweat scraper tool to remove lather from a sweating horse.

tick very small insect that attaches itself to a larger animal and feeds on it.

Further Resources

Books

Gottlieb, Beth. *I Love Horses!* New York, NY: Gareth Stevens Publishing, 2023

Jeffries, Corina. *We Can Draw Horses*. New York, NY: Windmill Books, 2023.

Smith, Robyn. *Horse Life: The Ultimate Guide to Caring for and Riding Horses for Kids*. Emeryville, CA: Rockridge Press, 2021.

Websites

10 Fun Facts About Horses
spca.bc.ca/news/fun-facts-about-horses/
Discover more fun facts about horses, including information about their senses and smarts.

Horses
www.dkfindout.com/us/animals-and-nature/horses/
Learn more about horses and their amazing abilities.

Przewalski's Horse
kids.nationalgeographic.com/animals/mammals/facts/przewalskis-horse
Explore more about this wild horse.

Publisher's note to parents and teachers: Our editors have reviewed the websites listed here to make sure they're suitable for students. However, websites may change frequently. Please note that students should always be supervised when they access the internet.

Index